Get Ready

Workbook

3

Author
LLS English Research Center

J PLUS
Language Publishing Co.

The Elephants Are On The Tenth Floor

Unit 1

Write down the numbers from first to tenth in order.

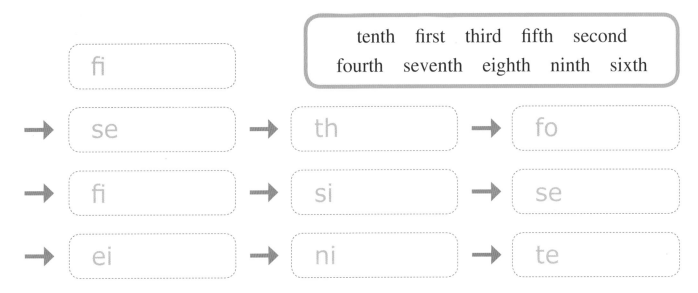

| fi |

tenth　first　third　fifth　second
fourth　seventh　eighth　ninth　sixth

→ | se | → | th | → | fo |

→ | fi | → | si | → | se |

→ | ei | → | ni | → | te |

Draw a line to complete the sentences.

May I　·　　　·　the 1st floor?

What's on　·　　　·　in the apartment?

How about　·　　　·　help you?

Do the tigers live　·　　　·　the kangaroos?

Translate into English.

사자들은 5층에 살아요.

the　on　5th　live
Lions　floor　.

_____

❀ **Fill in the blanks.**

____ ____ip   fi__ __   bru__ __

🌀 **Fill in the blanks.**

   Five _____ are on the ship.

   Wash your _____ .

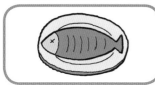   The _____ is on the dish.

   She is wearing a new _____ .

◢ **Circle the pictures that have <u>sh</u> sound.**

I Have A Headache

❋ Match and trace.

- • toothache

- • stomachache

- • fever

- • cough

- • headache

✔ Read and write in the numbers in order.

☐ I have a headache.

☐ What's wrong with you?

☐ Take care, Bob!

☐ That's too bad.

◎ Translate into English.

너 기침하니?

> have   a   you   Do   cough   ?

_____

Fill in the blanks.

pea__ __   __ __eese   sandwi__ __

Choose two words that have <u>ch</u> sound.

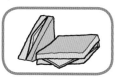   cheese / ship / sandwich / cough

   lunchbox / fish / brush / peach

   cheese / chicken / dish / wash

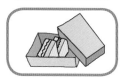   peach / skirt / shirt / chicken

Fill in the blanks.

__ __icken   pea__ __   di__ __   sandwi__ __

fi__ __   __ __air   lun__ __   __ __ip

He Is From Canada

Unscramble the words and write down the correct number of each nation.

OKARE

ERAIMAC

ANPAJ

NREACF

ANCIH

Trace and match.

Are you British? •
                  • Thank you. Bye!

Have a nice trip. •
                  • No, I'm not. I am French.

Where are you from? •
                  • I am from Canada.

Translate into English.

나는 한국에서 왔어.

I   from   Korea   am   .

Fill in the blanks.

__ __eat   __ __istle   __ __ale

Choose and fill in the blanks.

 The   wheat / weat   is a plant.

 The   wite / white   whale / wale   is in the sea.

 The   wale / whale   has a   wistle / whistle .

 The horse has a   wheel / weel .

Circle the correct words.

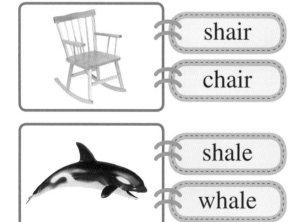 shair / chair   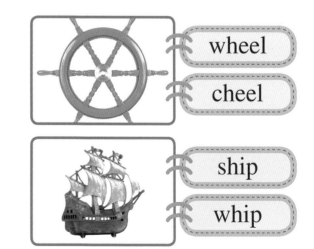 wheel / cheel

shale / whale   ship / whip

Go Straight And Turn Left

 Look at the pictures and write down the correct answers.

> Over there.   Go straight.
> Around the corner.   Turn right.

Where is the bank?

_____

_____

_____

_____

✔ **Number the sentences in order.**

☐ How can I get to the bakery?   ☐ Thank you!

☐ Excuse me.   ☐ Go straight and turn left.

◎ **Translate into English.**

버스 정류장이 어디니?

> bus stop   is   Where   the   ?

_____

Fill in the blanks.

__ __one

ele__ __ant

__ __oto

Match and trace the words.

elephant

earphone

photo

phone

Fill in the blanks.

gra__ __

sandwi__ __

__ __onics

__ __one

__ __eat

ele__ __ant

lun__ __

__ __oto

Unit 5 My Hobby Is Cooking

🍀 **Match.**

painting

reading books

flying kites

playing computer

listening to music

cooking

✔️ **Write down a proper question for each answer.**

How is it?	What are you making?	What is your hobby?

_____ ·············▶ Pancakes!

_____ ·············▶ My hobby is cooking.

_____ ·············▶ Good. It's yummy.

◎ **Translate into English.**

내 취미는 컴퓨터 게임 하는 거야.

_____

the   computer games   is
playing   My   hobby   .

🦋 **Fill in the blanks.**

 __ __is

 __ __ree

 ma__ __

🌀 **Fill in the blanks.**

That
three
thick
this
Thumbs

[   ] bears are fishing.

Look at [   ] big fish.

They say, " [   ] up!"

I like math. It is a [   ] book.

[   ] is a big bird.

◢ **Read and match.**

(PH)   (SH)   (CH)

(WH)   (TH)

How Much Is It?

Match.

rain •

sca •

teddy •

umb •

ha •

swimming •

• rella

rf •

• coat

• suit

t •

• bear

Write down the correct answers.

| I want to buy sunglasses. | Yeah, I'd like it. | It's 30 dollars. |

How much is it? ·············▶ _____

Do you want that? ·············▶ _____

May I help you? ·············▶ _____

Translate into English.

이 모자는 얼마예요?

much   is   hat   this   How   ?

_____

✿ **Fill in the blanks.**

__amera

__oat

fa__e

🌀 **Fill in the blanks.**

> circus   circle   cucumber   face

The _____ is not like a _____ .

The _____ is long.

There is a seal in the _____ .

🔺 **Match.**

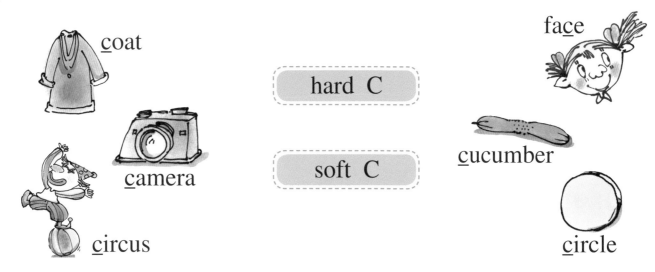

coat

camera

circus

hard C

soft C

face

cucumber

circle

It's Cold In Winter

 Complete the sentences.

| hot and sunny | cool and windy | nice and warm | cold and snowy |

Spring

It's _____ .

Summer

It's _____ .

Fall

It's _____ .

Winter

It's _____ .

◎ **Translate into English.**

겨울에는 날씨가 어떠니?

_____

weather   in   What's
like   winter   the   ?

✿ Fill in the blanks.

wa__on

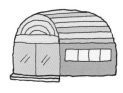

__ym

__oat

⑥ Match and trace.

dragon

goat

giraffe

wagon

Write down the words and circle the pictures that have <u>hard g</u> sound.

_____

_____

Where Do You Live?

🍀 **Write down the meaning of each word.**

live ➡ _____   find ➡ _____

help ➡ _____   go ➡ _____

phone ➡ _____   street ➡ _____

✔ **Fill in the blanks.**

1. _____ is the Apple Street?

2. I can't _____ my house.

3. What is your _____ ?

4. Let me _____ you find your home.

5. I _____ in 234 Apple Street.

6. My house is across _____ the office.

help
live
from
Where
find
phone number

◎ **Translate into English.**

너 어디에 사니?

live you Where do ?

_____

Fill in the blanks.

p__ __k   c__ __n   h__ __n   b__ __n

Match and trace.

• Let's go to the farm.

• There is a big worm.

• There is a giant corn.

Choose the correct words.

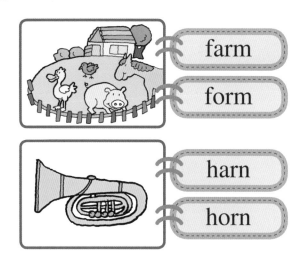

farm

form

born

barn

harn

horn

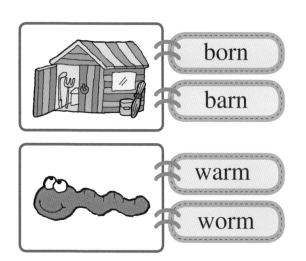

warm

worm

May I Speak To Megan?

Find the words and write.

pelcidspeakeowl ➡ ____ ____ ____ ____ ____

slekhelloksi ➡ ____ ____ ____ ____ ____

slelistenwxp ➡ ____ ____ ____ ____ ____ ____

lwehold ➡ ____ ____ ____ ____

lecpleasewo ➡ ____ ____ ____ ____ ____ ____

Number the sentences in order.

☐ May I speak to Megan?

☐ Hi, Megan.

☐ Hello! This is Tina.

☐ This is Megan speaking.

☐ Hello, this is Denny's residence.

Translate into English.

팸과 통화할 수 있나요?

Pam   to   speak   I   May   ?

_____

Fill in the blanks and read.

h__ __t

sing__ __

sh__ __t

Match and trace.

A farmer / farmur is wearing a short / shirt .

A tortle / turtle gets hurt / hort .

Fill in the blanks.

n__ __se

h__ __n

c__ __cle

p__ __k

h__ __t

f__ __mer

How Can I Go There?

 Write down the words using the given codes.

1	2	3	4	5
a	e	i	o	u

t r 5 c k

→ _____

1 3 r p l a n 2

→ _____

b 3 k 2

→ _____

m 4 t 4 r c y c l 2

→ _____

t r 1 3 n

→ _____

s 5 b w 1 y

→ _____

✔ **Make a sentence using verb "can".**

park / bus ➡ I can go to the park by bus.

school / bus

➡ _____

Hawaii / airplane

➡ _____

Pusan / train

➡ _____

◎ **Translate into English.**

거기에 어떻게 가니?

can   I   go   How   there   ?

_____

Fill in the blanks.

c__b__   k__t__   c__p__

 **Circle the correct answers.**

Tim flew a   kite / kit   .

Jane found a   pin / pine   tree.

Bill made a paper   plane / plan   .

Jin made ice   cubs / cubes   .

Match.

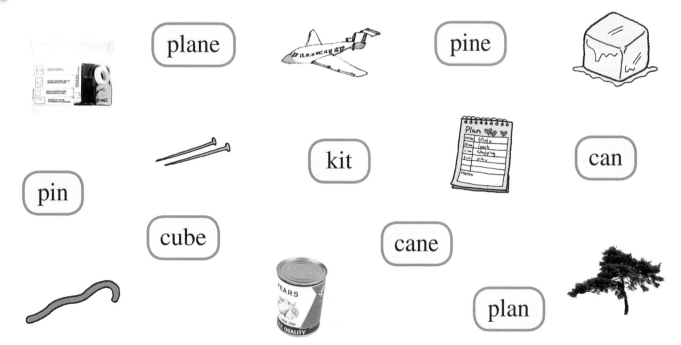

plane   pine

kit   can

pin

cube   cane

plan

Where Were You, Alice?

 Fill in the blanks.

| uncle's house   bookstore   zoo   park   movie theater   hospital |

_____   _____   _____

_____   _____   _____

Read and write the number in order.

Where **were** you?　　•　　• I am at the park.

What **are** you doing?　•　　• I was at the park.

Where **are** you?　　•　　• I am singing.

What **were** you doing? •　　• I was singing.

Translate into English.

너 어제 뭐하고 있었니?

_____

| yesterday   you   doing |
| were   What   ? |

Fill in the blanks.

lam__   cas__le   tom__   whis__le

 **Trace and match.**

castle  whistle

Christmas climb

Cross out every silent sound.

listen   climb

Christmas   thumb

castle   whistle

What A Big Mouth!

🍀 Match.

big   small   tall   beautiful   dirty

book   flower   hat   hand   tree

◎ Translate into English.

멋진 자전거구나!

a   bike   What   nice   !

_____

✿ **Fill in the blanks.**

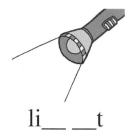

li__ __t

__rist

__ni__ __t

🌀 **Fill in the blanks.**

It is ⬚ .

The ⬚ ⬚ a letter.

In the moon⬚ .

His ⬚ is on his knee.

◢ **Cross out every silent sound.**

w r i s t	k n i g h t
c l i m b	n i g h t
c a s t l e	l i g h t
k n e e	l i s t e n

Write down the words using the given codes.

a	e	f	h	l	m	n	r	s	t
▨	☞	⊔	⊗	◿	⇀	◉	⬠	✳	⦀

✳☞☞ 　　　　　 ✳⇀☞◿◿ 　　　　　 ⊗☞▨⬠

＿＿＿＿＿　　　　 ＿＿＿＿＿　　　　 ＿＿＿＿＿

⦀▨✳⦀☞ 　　　　 ⊔☞☞◿ 　　　　 ✳☞◉✳☞

＿＿＿＿＿　　　　 ＿＿＿＿＿　　　　 ＿＿＿＿＿

Circle the words and draw them in the boxes in order.

dkl(eyes)kelcfingerslwogearsekdsnoselofsqtongueepwl

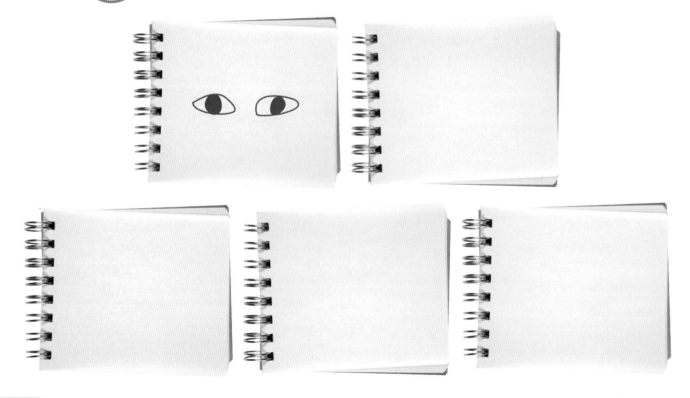

Unscramble the sentences.

1. I / my / with / taste / tongue / .

   ⇒ _____

2. see / my / with / I / eyes / .

   ⇒ _____

3. nose / my / smell / with / I / .

   ⇒ _____

Fill in the blanks.

| hear | smells | sounds | nose | ears | tastes |

I _____ with my _____ .

The drum _____ good.

I _____ with my _____ .

The pizza _____ good.

Don't Walk On The Grass

🍀 **Make a correct direction for each picture using the form "Don't"**

> Don't ~
>
> feed the fish
> pick the flower
> throw out the bottles
> walk on the grass
> touch the animal

_____

_____   _____

_____   _____

◎ **Translate into English.**

잔디를 밟으면 안돼!

> walk   on   Don't   the   grass   !

_____

Unscramble the sentences.

1. (fight / Don't / your / with / friend / .)

    ➡ _____

2. (on / Don't / the / write / desk / .)

    ➡ _____

3. (animal / touch / the / Don't / .)

    ➡ _____

Fill in the blanks.

| Don't   bottle   class   throw |

Don't _____ out the _____ .

_____ talk in the _____ .

I Am Taller Than You

Write the comparative form of each word.

tall

➡ _____

slow

➡ _____

fast

➡ _____

old

➡ _____

young

➡ _____

short

➡ _____

big

➡ _____

small

➡ _____

◉ Translate into English.

내가 너보다 빨라!

faster   you   than   I   am   .

_____

Unscramble the sentences.

1. shorter / than / am / I / you / .

   → _____

2. mine / gold / The / is / goose / !

   → _____

3. feet / My / than / bigger / are / yours / .

   → _____

Fill in the blanks.

| longer   mine   bigger   yours |

my eraser

your eraser

My eraser is _____ than

_____ .

your pencil

my pencil

Your pencil is _____ than

_____ .

Unit 16 — What Are You Going To Do?

🍀 **Make a sentence for each picture using the form "<u>be going to~</u>"**

I'm going to ~

do my homework
study English
play the piano
ride a bike
swim in a pool

_____

_____

_____

◎ **Translate into English.**

방과후에 무엇을 할 거니?

going   after   What   you
are   do   to   school   ?

_____

Rewrite each sentence using the form "<u>be going to</u>~"

> Jane / study English
>
> ➡ Jane is going to study <u>English.</u>

Max / read a book

➡ _____

Bob / watch T.V

➡ _____

Sue / have breakfast

➡ _____

 Unscramble the sentences.

1. what / to / do / they / are / going / ?

    _____

2. get / at / 8 / Max / going / is / to / up / .

    _____

Answers

Unit 1

Page 2

first − second − third − fourth − fifth − sixth − seventh − eighth − ninth − tenth

May I   the 1st floor?
What's on   in the apartment?
How about   help you?
Do the tigers live   the kangaroos?

Lions live on the 5th floor.

Page 3

ship   fish   brush

sheep / brush / fish / shirt

Unit 2

Page 4

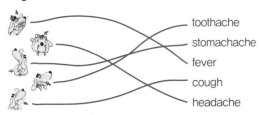

toothache
stomachache
fever
cough
headache

2−1−4−3

Do you have a cough?

Page 5

peach   cheese   sandwich

cheese   sandwich / lunchbox   peach
cheese   chicken / peach   chicken

chicken   peach   dish   sandwich
fish   chair   lunch   ship

Unit 3

Page 6

KOREA 1 / AMERICA 4 / JAPAN 3 / FRANCE 2 / CHINA 5

Are you British?   Thank you. Bye!
Have a nice trip.   No, I'm not. I am French.
Where are you from?   I am from Canada.

I am from Korea.

Page 7

wheat   whistle   whale

wheat / white − whale / whale − whistle / wheel

chair − wheel − whale − ship

Unit 4

Page 8

Around the corner. − Go straight. − Turn right. − Over there.

2−4−1−3

Where is the bus stop?

Page 9

phone   elephant   photo

elephant
earphone
photo
phone

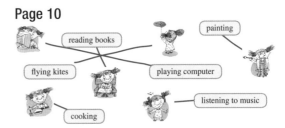

graph   sandwich   phonics   phone
wheat   elephant   lunch   photo

Unit 5

Page 10

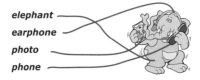

reading books   painting
flying kites   playing computer
cooking   listening to music

What are you making?
What is your hobby?
How is it?

My hobby is playing the computer games.

Page 11

this   three   math

Three / this / Thumbs / thick / That

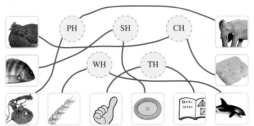

PH   SH   CH
WH   TH

Unit 6

Page 12

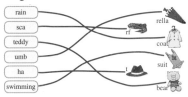

rain / sca / teddy / umb / ha / swimming

rella / rf / coat / t / suit / bear

It's 30 dollars. / Yeah, I'd like it. / I want to buy sunglasses.

How much is this hat?

Page 13

camera   coat   face

face – circle – cucumber – circus

hard C – camera coat / soft C – circus cucumber face circle

Unit 7

Page 14

It's nice and warm. / It's hot and sunny.
It's cool and windy. / It's cold and snowy.

What's the weather like in winter?

Page 15

wagon   gym   goat

dragon   **goat**
giraffe   **wagon**

goat dragon giant
wagon giraffe gym

Unit 8

Page 16

살다 찾다 / 돕다 가다 / 전화 거리

Where / find / phone number / help / live / from

Where do you live?

Page 17

park   corn   horn   barn

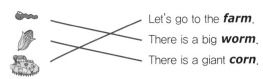

Let's go to the **farm**.
There is a big **worm**.
There is a giant **corn**.

farm barn horn worm

Unit 9

Page 18

speak / hello / listen / hold / please

3–5–2–4–1

May I speak to Pam?

Page 19

hurt   singer   shirt

farmer   shirt / turtle   hurt

nurse horn circle / park hurt farmer

Unit 10

Page 20

truck   airplane   bike / motorcycle   train   subway

I can go to school by bus.
I can go to Hawaii by airplane.
I can go to Pusan by train.

How can I go there?

Page 21

cube   kite   cape

kite / pine / plane / cubes

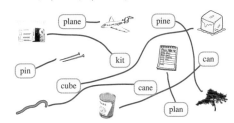

plane pine
pin kit can
cube cane
plan

Unit 11

Page 22

zoo   uncle's house   hospital / movie theater   bookstore   park

Where were you?   I am at the park.
What are you doing?   I was at the park.
Where are you?   I am singing.
What were you doing?   I was singing.

What were you doing yesterday?

Page 23

lamb   castle   tomb   whistle

castle   **whistle**
Christmas   **climb**

Answers

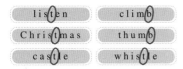

li**s**(t)e n	c l i m(b)
C h r i s(t)m a s	t h u m(b)
c a s(t)l e	w h i s(t)l e

Unit 12

Page 24

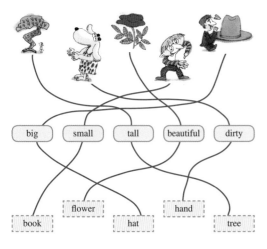

What a nice bike!

Page 25

light   wrist   knight

night / knight / writes − light / wrist

(w)r i s t	(k)n i(g)h t
c l i m(b)	n i(g)h t
c a s(t)l e	l i(g)h t
(k)n e e	l i**s**(t)e n

Unit 13

Page 26

see   smell   hear
taste   feel   sense

fingers   ears   nose   tongue

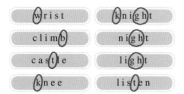

Page 27

I taste with my tongue.
I see with my eyes.

I smell with my nose.
hear − ears − sounds − smell − nose − tastes

Unit 14

Page 28

Don't feed the fish. / Don't pick the flower.
Don't walk on the grass. / Don't throw out the bottles.
Don't touch the animal.

Don't walk on the grass!

Page 29

Don't fight with your friend.
Don't write on the desk.
Don't touch the animal.

Don't throw out the bottle.
Don't talk in the class.

Unit 15

Page 30

taller   slower
faster   older
younger   shorter
bigger   smaller

I am faster than you.

Page 31

I am shorter than you.
The gold goose is mine.
My feet are bigger than yours.

My eraser is bigger than yours.
Your pencil is longer than mine.

Unit 16

Page 32

I'm going to play the piano.
I'm going to ride a bike.
I'm going to study English.
I'm going to swim in a pool.
I'm going to do my homework.

What are you going to do after school?

Page 33

Max is going to read a book.
Bob is going to watch T.V.
Sue is going to have breakfast.

What are they going to do?
Max is going to get up at 8.